STARTING

The Human Body

Written by Sally Hewitt

W

FRANKLIN WATTS

First published in 2010 by Franklin Watts
338 Euston Road, London NW1 3BH

Franklin Watts Australia
Level 17/207 Kent Street, Sydney NSW 2000

Editor: Katie Dicker
Art Direction: Rahul Dhiman (Q2AMedia)
Designer: Shruti Aggarwal (Q2AMedia)
Picture researcher: Anju Pathak (Q2AMedia)
Craft models made by: Shruti Aggarwal (Q2AMedia)
Photography: Divij Singh (Q2AMedia)

Picture credits:
t=top b=bottom c=centre l=left r=right

Cover: Pete Saloutos/Photolibrary, Jaimie
Duplass/Istockphoto, Utekhina Anna/Shutterstock.
Title page: Pedro Talens Masip/Shutterstock.
Insides: Catherine Yeulet/Istockphoto: 6, Muzsy/
Shutterstock: 7t, Patrick Hermans/Shutterstock: 7b,
Maximilian Stock Ltd/Science Photo Library: 8t, Julian
Rovagnati/Istockphoto: 8b, Martin Spurny/Shutterstock,
Eileen Hart/Istockphoto: 10, Judy Barranco/Istockphoto:
11t, Zhu Difeng/Shutterstock, Anton Albert/Shutterstock,
Yuri Arcurs/Shutterstock, Distinctive Images/
Shutterstock, Zsolt Nyulaszi/Shutterstock: 11b, John
Woodcock/Istockphoto: 12, Avava/Shutterstock: 13t,
Pablo Eder/Shutterstock: 13br, Laurence Mouton/
Photolibrary: 14t, Leonard Lessin/Photolibrary: 14b,
Radius Images/Photolibrary: 16t, Photolibrary: 16b,
Imagesource/Photolibrary: 18t, Pedro Talens Masip/
Shutterstock: 18b, Erproductions Ltd/Photolibrary: 20t,
Oguz Aral/Shutterstock: 20b, Corbis/Photolibrary: 22t,
Paco Ayala/Photolibrary: 22b, Joe Belanger/Istockphoto:
23t, Emin Ozkan/Shutterstock: 23b, Juan Silva/Getty
Images: 24t, Marcos Welsh/Photolibrary: 26t, Steve
Rabin/Istockphoto: 26b, Rene Jansa/Shutterstock: 27tl,
Carlush/Shutterstock: 27cl, Petrenko Andriy/
Shutterstock: 27bl, Jaimie Duplass/Istockphoto: 27c,
Utekhina Anna/Shutterstock: 27r.

Q2AMedia Image Bank: Cover, Imprint page,
Contents page, 9, 11, 13, 15, 17, 19, 23, 25.
Q2AMedia Art Bank: 21, 27.

With thanks to our model Shruti Aggarwal.

A CIP catalogue record for this book
is available from the British Library.

ISBN: 978 0 7496 8763 2

Dewey Classification: 612'22

Printed in China

Franklin Watts is a division of Hachette Children's Books,
an Hachette UK company.
www.hachette.co.uk

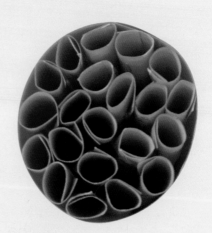

Contents

Words that appear in **bold** can be found in the glossary on pages 28–29.

Your body

You are a type of animal called a human. Humans have a body with parts that work together so you can grow, learn, eat and drink, **breathe** and move around.

Different and the same

Everyone is unique, which means no two people are exactly the same. Your shape and size, the colour of your skin, eyes and hair and the sound of your voice are some of the things that help people to recognise you. We are all unique, but our bodies work in the same way and we all need the same things to stay healthy, to learn and to grow.

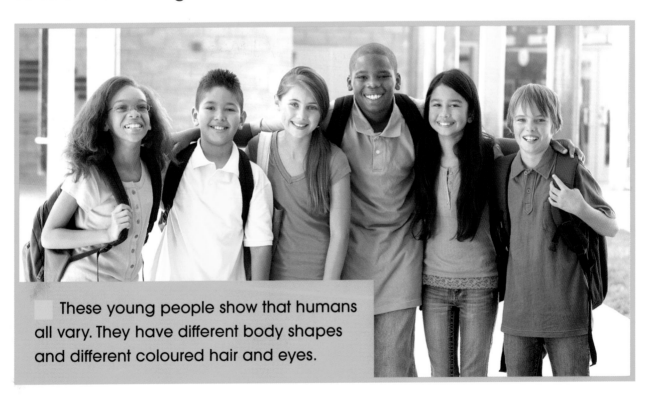

These young people show that humans all vary. They have different body shapes and different coloured hair and eyes.

A healthy body

Your body needs water, food, exercise and rest to be healthy. You can help to keep your body healthy by drinking plenty of water, choosing food that is good for you, keeping active and making sure that you get enough sleep.

When you exercise, you help your body to be healthy and strong.

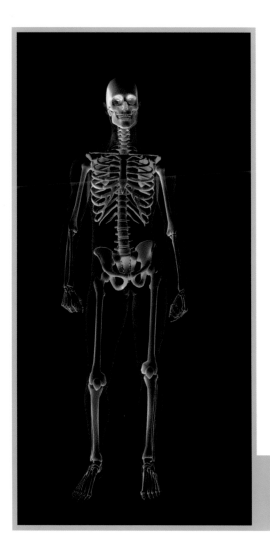

Under the skin

Under your skin is a **skeleton** made up of bones. Your bones protect the soft **organs** inside you. Each organ has a particular job to do. Your lungs, for example, are organs that help you to breathe and your stomach is an organ that helps you to **digest** food. With the help of your brain, your organs work together to keep you alive and well.

This X-ray picture shows a person's skeleton under the skin.

A healthy body

If you have a healthy body, you feel well. A healthy body is always growing and repairing itself. It fights **germs** and heals itself if it is hurt. To do this, it uses a lot of **energy**.

Healthy eating

Food is the fuel your body burns to give you energy. Fruit and vegetables keep your skin and bones healthy. Bread, pasta and cereals give you energy. Meat, fish, cheese and nuts help your body to grow and repair itself. You need a little sugar, salt and fat every day. Your body also needs plenty of water.

This diagram shows the different types of food you need to eat to be healthy.

Exercise makes you hot and thirsty, so you need to drink water when you are active.

Exercise and rest

Exercise, such as swimming, cycling and running, helps to keep your body healthy. It makes your heart and lungs work hard and keeps your bones and muscles strong. Your body works hard all day, so rest is important, too.

Design a 'Let's keep healthy' leaflet

What would you put in a leaflet giving children and adults ideas on how to keep healthy?

Here are some examples you could include:

Food

- Choose water instead of sugary drinks when you are thirsty.
- Try a new healthy food once a week.

Exercise

- Walk or cycle to school at least once a week.
- Learn a new skill such as swimming, cycling or skipping.
- Take your dog for a walk (if you have one) or take your mum, dad or grandparents for a walk!

Rest

- Curl up with a good book.
- Allow your body to rest after a meal, before you get active again.

Eat at least five portions of fruit and vegetables every day.

Make sure you get plenty of sleep to be ready for the new day ahead.

Brain and nerves

Your brain is the part of the body you learn with and it controls everything you do. Instructions are carried between your brain and the parts of your body along pathways called **nerves**.

Brain power

Your brain is soft. It is protected by your skull, the strong bone that gives your head its shape. Each part of your brain has a job to do. You use your brain to think. Your brain also controls the workings of your body.

Sending messages

Nerves run from your brain along your spinal cord and spread out around your body. Messages travel along your nerves to tell your brain what your body is doing. Your brain sends messages back to tell your body how to react.

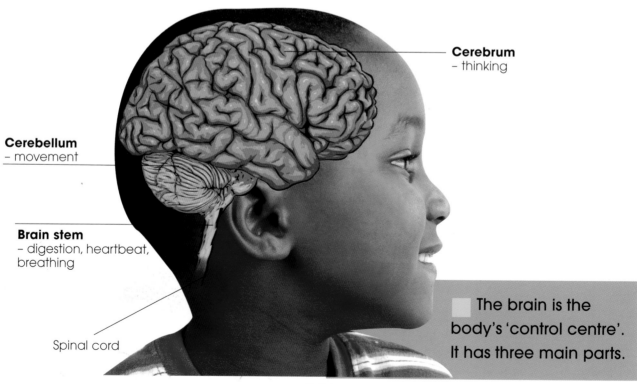

Cerebrum
– thinking

Cerebellum
– movement

Brain stem
– digestion, heartbeat, breathing

Spinal cord

The brain is the body's 'control centre'. It has three main parts.

10

Riding a bike is a skill that you need to practise.

Learning new skills

You learn new skills when your brain remembers something new. When you learn to ride a bike, for example, practice helps your brain to learn how to do it. Messages pass from your body to your brain and back again, until the new skill becomes easier.

Test your memory

You will need:
- card • scissors • 10 pictures of faces cut from magazines
- glue • pen • timer

1 Cut out ten playing card-sized rectangles and ten strips of card the same width. Stick a face on each card.

2 Make up a name for every face and write it on the back of the card and again on a strip of card.

3 Lay out five cards, face upwards. Put their name card under each one.

4 Ask a friend to study the cards for one minute. Then lay the five cards and names down again in a different order. Can your friend match the faces to the names? Check the name on the back of each card.

Mrs. McDuff   Otis   Peter   Maya   Mr. Brown

5 Shuffle the cards and lay out six or more. Is it easier when your friend has seen the cards before?

Heart and circulation

The heart and **blood vessels** are the organs that carry blood all around your body. This movement is called circulation. Your blood delivers **oxygen** and goodness from your food, called **nutrients**, and collects **waste**.

Beating heart

Your heart is a powerful muscle. It squeezes itself to push blood around your body. Your heart has two pumps. The left pump sends blood full of oxygen through blood vessels called arteries to your whole body.

When it has delivered the oxygen and nutrients, the blood travels back through blood vessels called veins into the right pump. From here it is pumped into the lungs to collect oxygen again.

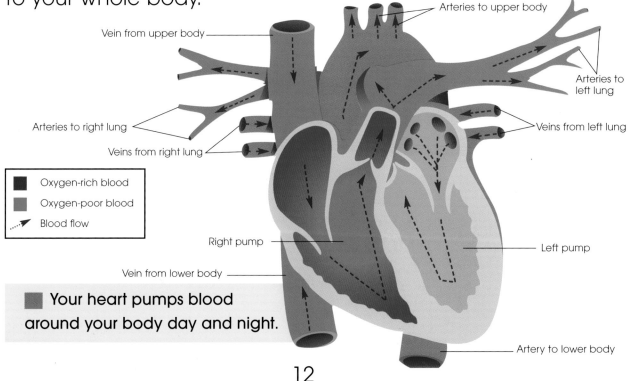

Vein from upper body

Arteries to upper body

Arteries to left lung

Arteries to right lung

Veins from left lung

Veins from right lung

■ Oxygen-rich blood
■ Oxygen-poor blood
⋯➤ Blood flow

Right pump

Left pump

Vein from lower body

Artery to lower body

■ Your heart pumps blood around your body day and night.

12

Your pulse rate tells you how fast your heart is beating.

Feeling your pulse

Every time your heart pumps blood into your arteries, they bulge a little. You can feel this 'pulse' in the arteries in your wrist and neck. When you exercise, your body needs extra oxygen and nutrients from your blood, so your heart beats faster. When you are resting, your heart beats more slowly.

Take and 'see' your pulse

You will need:
- blob of poster putty
- drinking straw • timer

1 Find the pulse in your wrist by feeling for it with the fingers of your other hand.

2 Push the blob of poster putty gently onto the spot where the pulse feels strongest, so it stays in place. Now push one end of the straw into the putty so it stands upright.

3 Lie your arm flat on a table and watch the straw twitch with each pulse beat. How many times does the straw twitch in one minute?

Take your pulse at different times of day. For example, when you have just woken up, after running upstairs or after a meal. What differences do you notice?

Breathing

Oxygen is a gas in the air that your body needs to stay alive. Your nose, **airways**, lungs and breathing muscles are the organs that you use to breathe in oxygen and take it into your body.

In and out

You breathe in (inhale) air through your nose and mouth. It goes down your **windpipe** and into your lungs where the oxygen passes into your blood. A waste gas called **carbon dioxide** passes from your blood to your lungs. You breathe out (exhale) this gas.

When you breathe out, your warm, moist breath mists up a cold window.

You can see the air from your lungs when you blow up a balloon.

Breathing muscles

Your breathing muscles work automatically to pull and push air in and out of your lungs. When you breathe in, muscles widen your chest and lungs to suck air in. When you breathe out, your chest and lungs get smaller and push air out again.

Make a model lung

Ask an adult to help you with this activity

You will need:
• 2 litre plastic bottle • balloon
• plastic bag • scissors
• elastic band • strong tape

1 Ask an adult to cut the top third off the plastic bottle and remove the lid.

2 Pull the open end of the balloon over the bottle spout. Push the balloon down inside the bottle.

3 Cut a circle of plastic from the plastic bag, bigger than the cut end of the bottle. Cover the open end of the bottle with the plastic and fix it with an elastic band.

Now tape it firmly in place with strong tape.

4 With your thumb, push the plastic up gently to make less space around the balloon. Watch the balloon shrink as air goes out of it. Now release the pressure to make more space around the balloon and watch air move back into it.

The balloon is like your lungs – they fill when the space around them expands (gets bigger) and empty when the space around them contracts (gets smaller).

Skeleton and bones

Your skeleton is a strong frame. A fully grown human has 206 bones. Your skeleton holds you upright, gives you your shape and allows you to move. It protects soft organs such as your brain, heart and lungs.

Bones

A baby's bones are soft and flexible. As you grow, your bones become harder. Bones are light and strong. The outside layer is smooth and hard. The middle layer looks like a sponge. If you break a bone, over time it can mend itself.

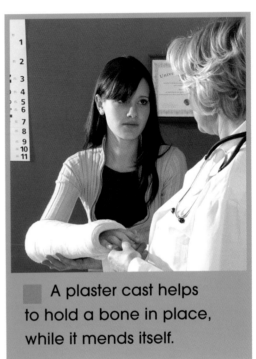

A plaster cast helps to hold a bone in place, while it mends itself.

Your joints bend and swivel to move your body in different ways.

Joints

The bones in your skeleton are joined together in places called joints. Many joints move. Your elbows, knees and fingers have **hinge joints**. They bend and straighten like the hinge of a door. Your hip and shoulder joints swivel in every direction.

Make a model bone and test its strength

You will need:
- coloured A4 paper
- scissors • sticky tape
- paperback books

1 Cut two pieces of A4 paper into thirds lengthways to get six strips of paper about 21 cm x 10 cm. Roll one strip into a short tube, and fix it with sticky tape.

2 Stand the tube upright on a flat surface. Place a book across the top of it. How many books will the tube hold before it collapses? Remake the tube if needed.

3 Cut the remaining paper strips lengthways to make smaller strips about 4 cm x 10 cm. Roll each one into a long tube and fix with sticky tape.

4 Pack the inside of the large tube with the smaller tubes standing upright. Test the tube for strength again. How many books can it support before it collapses this time?

The new tube is much stronger. Like a bone, it is also light. It has a hard outside and closely-packed tubes inside. The tubes strengthen the bone, but keep it light.

Muscles and movement

Your body is moved by muscles. Muscles move your bones by pulling them. You use muscles in your face to smile, frown and blink. Your heart is a muscle that pumps blood around your body.

Moving around

Strong cords called tendons attach muscles to your bones. Some muscles are attached to two bones, stretched across a joint. When you bend your knees, for example, different muscles move your legs and flex your knee joints.

Biceps muscle

When you flex your arm, the muscles called biceps in the top of your arm tense and shorten.

Strong muscles

Muscles that you use a lot can become bigger and stronger. Those you don't use much can become smaller and weaker. Skiers and cyclists have strong muscles in their legs. You can keep your muscles strong and healthy by getting plenty of exercise.

Strong muscles in the legs of cyclists help them to pedal faster.

Play 'bend and balance'

A game for two players to test your muscle strength and balance.

You will need:
- sheet of A4 white card
- 4 sheets of A3 coloured card and 4 sheets of A4 coloured card (red, yellow, blue and green) • scissors • pen • ruler

1 Using the A4 card, cut four playing card-sized pieces of white card and four each of red, yellow, blue and green card. Cut a circle about 28 cm across from each piece of A3 coloured card.

2 On the white cards write:
   i) right foot ii) left foot
   iii) right hand iv) left hand

   Shuffle the white cards and put them face down in a pile. Shuffle the coloured cards and put them in a pile next to the white cards.

3 Player 1 stands on some grass, or a soft mat, with the four coloured circles around him or her. Player 2 picks up a white card (e.g. 'right hand'), then picks up a coloured card (e.g. 'green'). Player 1 puts their right hand on the green circle.

4 Player 2 calls out all the white cards, with a colour, and player 1 follows the instructions. Keep calling the cards until player 1 loses their balance and falls over! Then swop over.

The winner is the player who can make the most moves without losing their balance.

Digestion

When you eat, your body breaks down your food into tiny pieces. This process is called digestion. Nutrients from your food are sent all around your body in your blood. Nutrients give your body energy to work, grow and repair itself.

Teeth and chewing

Your food's journey starts in your mouth. First, you chew your food into small pieces. You need strong, healthy teeth for chewing. You should clean your teeth carefully and visit your dentist regularly.

You should clean your teeth after breakfast and last thing at night.

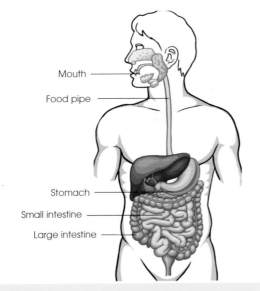

Mouth

Food pipe

Stomach

Small intestine

Large intestine

This diagram shows the main parts of the digestive system.

The journey

When you swallow your food, muscles squeeze it through a tube into your stomach. Your food is mashed into a runny soup. It moves to the small intestine where most nutrients pass to your blood. In the large intestine, water is absorbed to produce waste called **faeces**.

Make a digestion diary

Find out how long it takes for you to feel hungry again after you have eaten.

You will need:
- notebook • pencil • ruler
- pens or coloured pencils

1 Make a grid on the first page of your notebook, like the one shown below, and fill it in. Make a similar page for two or three days of the week.

Write a story of the journey of one of your meals.

Amazing journeys - starring... my breakfast!

I ate breakfast too quickly and didn't chew my food properly so I got hiccups. It lasted half an hour! Lumpy food went down my food pipe and into my stomach where...

	Monday		
	Time	**Food**	**Comment**
breakfast	7:00	 cereal, banana, orange juice	Ate too quickly – hiccups!
hungry	10:15	✗✗✗	✗✗✗
snack	10:30	 bran muffin, milk	School cookery club muffins. Yum!
hungry	12:30	✗✗✗	Football practice. Starving!
lunch	12:45	meat pie, beans, fruit yoghurt, water 	Nice and filling.
hungry	✗✗✗	✗✗✗	✗✗✗
snack	✗✗✗	✗✗✗	✗✗✗
hungry	✗✗✗	✗✗✗	✗✗✗
supper	✗✗✗	✗✗✗	✗✗✗

Skin

Your skin is your body's biggest organ. Like all the organs in your body, it has particular jobs to do. It covers and protects your whole body and gives you your **sense** of touch.

In the Sun

Our skin colour is caused by a natural colour (or pigment) called melanin. It helps to protect us from the Sun's rays. Our skin makes more melanin in sunlight and turns darker. But too much Sun can burn and damage our skin. People from warm countries have more melanin in their skin for protection.

Sun cream protects our skin from the Sun's rays.

Police take fingerprints to prove who was at a crime scene.

Amazing skin

Your skin renews and repairs itself all the time. An outer layer of dead skin falls off when your skin rubs against your clothes or when you wash. Look at your fingertips through a magnifying glass and you will see fine lines called fingerprints. No two people in the world have the same fingerprints.

Take fingerprints

You will need:
- pencils • sharpener with a pot for shavings • 3 sheets of A4 white card • ruler
- black pen
- double-sided sticky tape
- scissors
- magnifying glass

1 Collect pencil shavings in the sharpener pot. Tip the shavings onto a sheet of card. Collect the pencil dust.

2 On each remaining sheet of card, draw two rows of five boxes. Label the top row 'Left hand' and the bottom row 'Right hand'. Write your name on one card, and your friend's name on the other.

3 Stick a small piece of double-sided sticky tape

to each square. Keep the protective paper on the top side.

4 Press the fingertip of your little finger into the black pencil dust. Pull off the protective paper from the first square and press your blackened fingertip onto the sticky tape. Take a print of all your fingers in the same way.

5 Stick your friend's fingerprints to the other card. Examine them with a magnifying glass.

Secretly make a fingerprint on another piece of sticky tape. Can your friend match it to the correct fingerprint on your card?

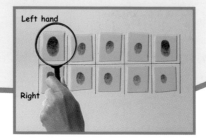

23

Senses

Your body has five senses – sight, hearing, smell, touch and taste. They tell you what is going on around you. You sense things with different parts of your body.

■ When you eat toast, you use all five senses to know it is good to eat.

You **see** the shape and colour

You **hear** it crunch

You **smell** a delicious smell

You **taste** it

You **feel** it is warm

Sense organs

We see with our eyes, hear with our ears, smell with our noses, touch and feel with our skin and taste with our tongues. Information detected by these **sense organs** is turned into signals that are flashed to the brain to tell us what is happening.

Keeping safe

Our senses help us to keep safe. We use our eyes and ears to see and hear traffic so we can cross the road safely. We feel heat coming from a fire so we know not to touch it. A bad smell tells us to keep away from harmful germs. A nasty taste tells us when our food is off.

Make a sensory sock-puppet

Ask an adult to help you with this activity

Make a toy to entertain a young child using sight, sound, movement and touch.

You will need:
- brightly coloured ankle sock
- pieces of brightly coloured felt • scissors • needle and thread • scraps of material and wool • small paper bag

1 Turn the sock so the sole is facing upwards. Push your hand inside so the heel is on top of your hand. Push the toe of the sock back between your fingers and thumb to make a mouth.

2 Cut ears, eyes and a nose from the pieces of felt. Ask

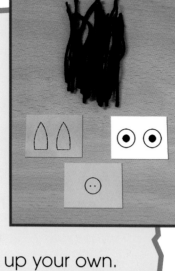

an adult to help you sew them onto the sock. You can copy the shapes shown here, or make up your own.

3 Sew on scraps of material with interesting textures and wool for hair.

4 Put your hand inside the paper bag and pull the sock over

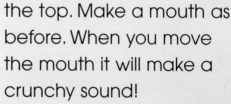

the top. Make a mouth as before. When you move the mouth it will make a crunchy sound!

Entertain a child you know with your sensory puppet! Let them touch it to feel the different textures.

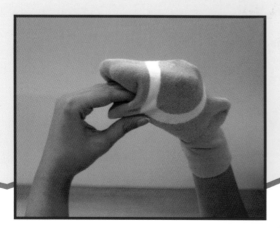

Life cycle

Human babies are born and they grow up into children. Children become adults and they may begin new **life cycles** by having children of their own. Over time, adult humans grow older and eventually die.

Growing up

A human baby starts life inside its mother's **womb**. After about nine months, it is ready to be born. A baby needs to be looked after all the time. It grows into a toddler and learns to walk and talk. Children go to school and learn to do many more things.

This mother is helping her one-year-old child to learn to walk.

Older people can teach children and young people a lot of new things.

Getting older

As adults get older, they start to change in several ways. Hair colour fades and skin becomes lined. Muscles and bones become weaker. Older people have a lot to offer. They have learned a great deal during their lives.

Make a personal album

Keep a record of growing up.

You will need:
- album or scrap book
- photographs of yourself
- scissors • sticky tape
- glue • pens • ruler
- coloured paper
- height chart

1 Collect photographs of yourself growing up. Stick them in the album in order and label them with your age and when they were taken. Find out facts about yourself and write them in. For example, how much you weighed at birth and when your first tooth grew.

2 On a new page, stick a photograph of yourself now. Write in your height, weight, how many teeth you have, and your favourite things such as your favourite colour, book, music, sport, etc.

3 Add a new page every few months or on every birthday.

4 Record your growth on a height chart and see how much you grow each year.

Look back through your album. How much have you changed over the years?

Glossary

airways

Airways are the tubes that connect your nose and throat to your lungs. The air you breathe in and out travels through your airways.

blood vessels

Blood vessels are tubes that carry blood through your heart and all around your body.

breathe

To breathe is to take air into your lungs and to let it out again. We need to breathe to stay alive.

carbon dioxide

Carbon dioxide is a gas in the air. Your body does not need carbon dioxide so you get rid of it when you breathe out.

digest

When your body digests food, it breaks it down, uses the goodness from it and gets rid of waste.

energy

Energy is the power to do work. Food, water and oxygen give your body the energy it needs to grow and work.

faeces

Faeces is the solid waste from your food that your body gets rid of when you go to the toilet.

germ

Tiny germs in the air or in food can cause diseases that make you ill if they get into your body.

hinge joint

A hinge joint lets bones open and shut in one direction, like the hinge of a door.

life cycle

A life cycle describes the way life goes round and round like a circle. Humans are born, they grow, they make new life like themselves so life can go on, and they die.

nerves

Nerves are pathways that carry messages between your brain and your body.

nutrients

Nutrients are the parts of your food that your body uses to grow, keep healthy and repair itself.

organ

An organ is a part of your body that has a particular job to do. For example, your lungs are the organs that you use to breathe.

oxygen

Oxygen is a gas in the air. Your body takes in oxygen when you breathe air into your lungs.

sense

A sense is one of the five ways you pick up information from the world around you. Your five senses are seeing, hearing, tasting, touching and smelling.

sense organs

Your sense organs are the parts of your body you use to sense the world around you – your eyes, ears, tongue, skin and nose.

skeleton

A skeleton is a frame made up of bones. It gives humans their shape and protects parts of their body.

waste

Waste is what is left over and not wanted. For example, a waste gas is what we breathe out when oxygen has been taken out of the air we breathe into our lungs.

windpipe

Your windpipe is a tube between your throat and your lungs. Air travels through your windpipe when you breathe.

womb

A womb is the part of a woman's body where a baby grows before it is ready to be born.

Index